A KINDNESS I WILL NEVER FORGET
A Young Widow's Story

by
Lisa Ramelow

Copyright © 2021 by Lisa Ramelow

All rights reserved.

No part of this book may be reproduced in any form or by any electronic or mechanical means, including information storage and retrieval systems, without written permission from the author, except for the use of brief quotations in a book review.

Printed in the United States of America

First Printing, 2021

Cover Design by Jennifer Schafer

ACKNOWLEDGMENTS

I would like to thank all those who have been reading my stories about "every day life," from the time I first began writing them, in 2011. You followed along with my "3AM insomnia reports," the stories about my treasured "kids" who worked for me in my restaurant business, and you cheered on my love of all things shoes, and my sport of parade walking in tall red high heels.

Your continual support of my writing, my business, and of my family, has been immeasurable to me. You have all inspired me to continue, and to publish this memoir.

CONTENTS

Foreword	vi
1. The Mailman	1
2. The Kitchen Floor	5
3. The Jacket	8
4. The Blue Eyes	12
5. A Difference in Families	16
6. The Calls	23
7. A Mother's Love	27
8. The Decisions	32
9. Standing on My Porch	37
10. Losing It	41
11. Bunkey and the Coffee Pot	45
12. The Long Walk	48
13. The Baby was Hungry	52
14. Dr. Jekyll and Mr. Ramelow	56
15. Wise Men Say	59
16. Sweet Laughter	65
17. Pretending	70
18. Re-enacting	77
19. The book, "Widowed"	81
20. The Grief Group	85
21. Anger? Not Me	88
22. I Need a Teenager	92
23. The Dreams	95
24. Slow Dancing on his Grave	99
25. The Widow Card	103
26. Death vs. Divorce	106
27. He Wasn't Perfect	110
28. A Glimmer of Hope	116
29. The Private Fan Club	121

30. Taking Him With Us	126
31. Continuing into Acceptance	132
32. The Opportunity	139
33. Real Acceptance	145
34. Thoughts on Grieving	149
Love from Ryan	155
Love from Hannah	157
About the Author	158

FOREWORD

January 3rd will always be significant to me.

It has been a very long time since that day in 1991, when I very suddenly became widowed, with a toddler and an infant, at just age 33.

And yet, even after 30 years, I still remember so very clearly each and every one of the moments expressed in these chapters.

I was very grateful to those who helped me. Each of these moments was "a kindness I will never forget," no matter how small the gesture may have seemed. These memories never left me.

I also learned of the great sense of determination I had within me.

This day no longer brings me sadness or despair. I found my way back to living a full and complete life. This is the story of how I made that happen.

It was suggested that I begin with the moral of the story.

When I looked up "moral" for more clarification, it said, "it was the lesson learned."

I learned way too many lessons from this for me to write just one here.

The definition also said the reader could interpret the moral themselves, based on what they had experienced in their own life.

I know I am not alone in feeling loss and deep pain, and of living through difficult times. And so, I will leave that to you, dear reader, to find your own moral to this story.

With love, Lisa

PS This photo was taken on January 2, 1991. It's so sweet and smiley. I had no idea what was coming.

1

THE MAILMAN

I started to hate the mailman.

He came around 2PM every day, and when he put the mail through the slot in the door, it sounded like someone was coming home.

My two-year-old little boy, Ryan, would run towards the door.

"Mommy! Daddy's home!"

My heart would hurt so much.

For my son, "Daddy coming home" had been the highlight of his day. He adored his father - they had spent hours together every evening.

But he was so little, that he just kept forgetting what had happened a few weeks before.

So then I would have to start "the conversation" again.

"Oh honey. I'm so sorry. Remember what Mommy told you? Daddy can't come home anymore. He wants to come home, but he can't. Remember how he 'broke' on the floor? He loved you so very much, and he would come home to see you and 'New Baby' if he could." (We called his new little sister Hannah, "New Baby")

"Oh, OK, Mommy," Ryan would say. "Oh. The men couldn't fix Daddy. But Mommy, Daddy could fix anything!"

"I know. But they couldn't fix Daddy."

"But Mommy, where is Daddy now?"

"Honey, Daddy's in heaven. Up in the sky. Way up there."

I would gesture towards the sky. It wasn't really an honest response. I didn't have any concept of heaven at all, not really.

"Mommy! I know! Let's take a plane and go see Daddy!! Daddy took planes all the time!"

"I'm sorry honey. There is no plane that can take us to see Daddy. I promise you, Daddy did not want to leave you, ever. He loved you so very much. Please, please remember how much Daddy loved you."

I silently prayed. Please. Please remember him. Please. Please know he loved you. Please.

"OK Mommy. But I wish we could see Daddy."

"I know honey. I wish we could too."

"Mommy, you're crying again. Don't cry Mommy."

Every day it was like this.

A 2½-year-old has no concept of death.

I did not want my son to suffer and cry every day. I wanted Ryan to remember the unconditional love he had been given.

As the days progressed, he asked about his father less and less. And while it was nice to see him remain a cheerful little boy, my heart hurt knowing that he was growing further and further from ever being able to remember his father, and how devoted he had been to him and his sister.

And then, one day, my little boy stopped asking.

I know. I probably should have been relieved.

But I knew what this meant.

My little boy had forgotten his father.

That killed me even more.

I was a mess.

2

THE KITCHEN FLOOR

January 3rd, 1991

Just a week before had been the first Christmas for our 3-month-old baby daughter.

That Thursday was a cold and rainy day. I sat on the sofa in our family room, nursing the baby.

Walt had taken two days off, which was very rare for him. Hannah's baptism was scheduled for the upcoming weekend, and he wanted to get the yard ready and try out some new chicken recipes. He loved to barbecue.

He walked into the room that morning in his blue robe, on his way outside for his usual routine of checking on his garden and reading the paper.

He stopped and looked at me.

He asked, "Honey, are we in a fight?"

I started laughing, and said, "No, it's OK."

He smiled and went outside.

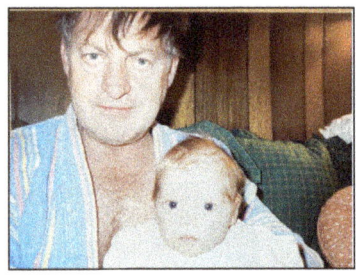

The truth was, I had been mad at him for a couple days over something dumb; I had basically stopped speaking to him. But I realized, if he hadn't noticed, then what was the point? So I stopped being mad. (Looking back, I thank God for this moment. I was so happy that we had "made up." It helped keep my sanity for what was to come).

When he came back in, he did something unusual.

He mentioned he was having really bad indigestion.

Walt never complained. And I mean EVER. He said his back hurt as well.

Then he shrugged and said, "No big deal," and went about his day.

My sister Teresa called. She wanted to get out of the house, so I told her to come over.

She arrived with her baby daughter, Rachel. We talked about going to lunch and decided on this pizza place where we could get a salad.

I almost left 2½-year-old Ryan at home with his dad, but decided to take him with us.

--

We were only gone about an hour. When we got back home, I opened the front door and carried Hannah inside in her car seat; I remember putting her down, and then turning back to say something to Teresa.

Ryan ran past me into the house, and on into the kitchen.

"Silly Daddy! Don't sleep on the floor Daddy!"

I looked toward my kitchen.

The refrigerator door was open. Walt was lying on the floor on his back, blue, and completely motionless.

I screamed, "Walt's on the floor!!" and ran towards him.

It felt like a tornado was exploding through my head and my body.

3
___

THE JACKET

I grabbed the phone as I knelt down over Walt; I was already dialing 9-1-1.

Teresa somehow got the babies out of their car seats and onto the sofa. She was trying to get Ryan to come over to her.

I was giving the operator my address "1-3-9…"

"Mommy, why is Daddy sleeping on the floor? Get up Daddy!"

I turned to Ryan. "Honey, Daddy isn't sleeping."

I don't know what made me say it, but I put it into words I thought a little boy would understand, "Honey, Daddy's broken. I'm trying to fix him."

At this moment I thought, "with just a little oxygen, he'll be fine."

Ryan ran back and forth from the kitchen to the living room. He kept asking why Daddy was broken, and was saying things like, "Mommy, can you fix Daddy? Will he wake up soon?"

The 9-1-1 operator was telling me how to do CPR. I was trying so hard to focus on what she was saying, as I alternated from blowing oxygen into his mouth, to doing compressions on his chest.

My heart raced and my hands shook.

I was filled with panic, but I continued to think that if I just got a little oxygen into him, he would be OK.

The operator asked if his chest was going up when I was breathing into his mouth. It wasn't. She reminded me to pinch his nostrils together first before delivering a breath.

Finally I did it exactly the way she told me. I blew a strong deep breath into his mouth and into his lungs.

I knew I had done it correctly this time, because I heard the most chilling sound I had ever heard; a sickening gurgling noise from within his body. I didn't know at the time what this meant, but his lungs had already filled up with fluid.

A sense of dread washed over me.

Within minutes, a lot of men entered my house carrying lots of equipment. I stepped back immediately from Walt, and they quickly knelt down beside him, communicating constantly with each other. I felt a little bit of relief watching them work. I remember taking a breath and thinking, "OK, they're here now. They're going to fix him. He's going to be OK."

I didn't want to think about the gurgling sound.

One of the men took out scissors and cut the sleeve of my husband's jacket in order to expose his vein, while another did CPR. I don't remember what else they were doing.

Somehow I realized that they would probably take him to a hospital and I would follow. I knew I couldn't leave Hannah for very long because I was nursing her and she would be hungry soon.

I scooped her up and pulled up my shirt and fed her while I continued to hover around the men on my kitchen floor.

My whole body trembled; I don't know how I held onto the baby.

"Is he going to be OK?

Is he going to be OK?"

Mostly, they (understandably) ignored me. But one of them looked up and said, "It doesn't look good ma'am."

I appreciated that.

It was a kindness I will never forget.

I was still holding onto the belief that he would be OK, and could be fixed if I just stayed calm and let them work on him. I wanted to believe that. I had to believe that.

But deep down, I really appreciated this man's honesty. It allowed me to see the tiniest speck of reality about what might happen.

They took him out on a gurney, and rushed him to a small local hospital.

I don't remember how, but I went in the transport with him.

--

I still have that jacket, the one he was wearing, the one the paramedic cut open. It was something I could never throw away. And never will.

4

THE BLUE EYES

I paced the floor in the very small waiting room of this little hospital.

I felt so desperate. I opened my wallet and took out two small photos of my children. I walked the floor holding them against my heart. I prayed to any God I could find, to please let Walt live. To please let my children have their father.

Then, a doctor and nurse approached me. The nurse held a box of tissues. I knew what was coming.

"We're so sorry," they said. "There was nothing we could do."

They told me I could see him. My hands were shaking as they led me to the little curtained-off area where he lay.

I had never had anyone close to me die before. And I had only seen a dead person once, from faraway, at a funeral.

This was all new to me. I always thought that it would be scary to be next to a dead person.

But, it wasn't.

They left me alone with him to say goodbye.

I stepped forward and looked down at him. I suddenly felt very peaceful.

He wasn't scary, because, he was my Walt.

I stood next to him and looked at him lying there motionless. I felt calm and my hands stopped shaking. I reached up and stroked his hair over and over again.

Tears poured out of my eyes as I quietly wept.

I talked to him.

"I'm so sorry honey. I know you didn't want to die. I know you don't want to leave us."

I just kept stroking his hair and kissing his face.

He had these huge, beautiful blue eyes, that both of our children had inherited. I wanted to see them one last time, so I gently opened them. His eyes were so vacant. I closed them.

"I'm so sorry honey."

I don't know how many times I said it.

I lay the pictures of our children on his chest.

"Don't worry honey. I will take good care of our babies. I promise you. I will do all the things that were important to you. I promise."

I felt frozen there and did not want to leave. But at some point, the nurse returned and let me know in a nice way, that it was time for me to go.

They needed me to give them the name of a mortuary to call to come get him.

A mortuary?

I was 33. I didn't know anything about mortuaries.

--

A man from the hospital drove me home. It wasn't far, but it felt like an eternity.

I walked in my front door and told my sister. She already expected it.

I picked up the baby to feed her.

My son ran over to hug me, "Mommy! You're home! Where's Daddy?"

I looked at my little boy who adored his father.

"Honey, do you remember the men who were in the kitchen, trying to fix Daddy?"

Ryan nodded yes.

"They couldn't fix Daddy. He can't come home."

"OK Mommy, so Daddy is coming home later?"

He didn't understand.

The emotions inside of me continued to feel like a raging tornado of disbelief and panic, but somehow I knew I needed to keep my composure at that moment.

I could feel the huge weight of responsibility ahead of me; there was no time to cry.

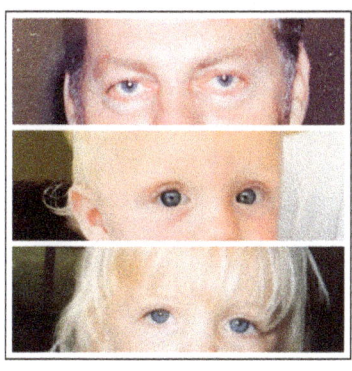

5

A DIFFERENCE IN FAMILIES

I was always worried that Walt would die before me. He was 22 years older than me.

Walt worked at Rockwell International in Downey, California; he supervised many projects of the Space Shuttle program, including the Tile Data Base and all the electrical systems.

He had a huge amount of responsibility, but always said, "Oh it's no big deal."

He wasn't fond of praise.

When I was 22 years old, I interviewed for an engineering job, and Walt was the person interviewing me.

I sat down in his office. He smiled warmly.

I don't remember the questions he asked me, but I felt like he understood me right away, like no one ever had before.

We had an instant mind meld.

He hired me to work on the Space Shuttle Tile Data Base.

After a few months, we began seeing each other, but kept our relationship quiet at work. After two years I transferred to another division so he would no longer be my direct boss.

--

Walt had three daughters from his previous marriage. He was so proud of them and couldn't wait for me to meet them.

I was nervous. They were teenagers, and I was in my 20's. What would they think? Would that be weird for them that I was closer in age to them, than to their father?

It wasn't. They didn't care about any of that. They just wanted their Dad to be happy.

At our wedding, they gave me a button that said, "New Mommy" along with a gold heart-shaped locket. It meant so much to me.

And they welcomed the birth of our each of our children, and were happy to have a little brother and a new sister.

This was in stark contrast to my family dynamic.

When Walt and I started dating, I didn't tell my parents about us for a while because I knew what would happen; it would be something far greater than disapproval. I knew my parents would be dead set against our age difference.

Walt was very matter-of-fact about it.

"Honey, don't worry, they'll be fine. People adjust once they know what they need to adjust to."

He thought the whole thing was ridiculous. He did not think our age difference was that big of a deal. And I don't think he quite understood how much influence my parents still had over me, and why their disapproval would affect me so strongly. He thought if there were any problems, they would blow over quickly.

It is embarrassing to admit, but my parents terrified me. I feared they would be successful in their efforts to break us up.

They were masters in emotional warfare. In our family, if you did not conform, not only were you shunned, but you were also emotionally ripped to pieces on the way out.

I had been on the receiving end of their wrath before, and it was excruciating. I didn't want to be in that place again.

When I finally told them that Walt and I were dating, they called me names, and told me how stupid I was to date an older man. They alternated between my mother crying, and my father yelling.

My mother made incredibly cruel comments about how disgusting I was to be with a man near my father's age. They said Walt was using me because he wanted to be with a younger woman, and that he didn't care about me as a person at all.

It was such an insult that they thought I was unable to sense somebody's real feelings towards me.

They were keenly aware that I was a sensitive person who still wanted their approval even though I was an adult. They made it clear that I was now a major disappointment to them, and that they would never come to any wedding, or have anything to do with any kids that we might have.

They refused to meet Walt, unable to accept our age difference. They hated him, without ever having met him.

My father had even said, "What if you have kids with him and then he dies? Then what?

I understood that my parents were worried about me. But they went too far.

After being together for five years, we decided to get married.

I called my parents and told them this news. They were not happy. They asked me to come over and said they just wanted to talk to me.

A few days later, I stopped over at their home.

When I got there, they reiterated their concerns about our age difference. They continued about how he was using me. It didn't matter to them that we had now been together for 5 years. They were not going to let this go and just accept it.

When they couldn't talk me out of it, they handed me a legal document.

They explained that they were writing me out of their will. They made it clear that their money would now be divided 3 ways, instead of 4.

My parents wanted their way, and they would do anything to win. It was bad enough to be handed the rewritten will, but even worse, was to see the looks on their faces.

They were smirking as if to say "we've got you now!" They looked triumphant. This was what they thought would convince me. They were sure they had "won." They actually believed that I would suddenly break off my plans just to get their money.

My heart sank.

Not because I wanted an inheritance. But because I couldn't believe how little they knew about me as a person. I was their daughter, and yet they looked so happy to be holding something over my head, something, with which they could "win."

It hurt deeply. I went ahead and planned my wedding without them.

--

Two days before my wedding, my father called me at work. "I just wanted to remind you that your mother and I won't be there."

He said it almost gleefully, with a cruel undertone; a last twist of the knife to "make me pay."

Despite all my parents had done to try to stop me, my wedding day was joyful.

My brother walked me down the aisle. My sisters stood up for me.

Everyone I cared about was there.

6

THE CALLS

My worst nightmare had just happened.

I had to keep my composure.

My sister looked after the babies while I got Ryan down for a nap.

I went into survival mode.

I knew I had to make a lot of calls, and none of them would be easy.

I don't why, but I called his boss first.

"Mr. Freddrick, this is Lisa Ramelow, Walt's wife. I need to tell you that Walt had a heart attack today."

I paused and took a breath to get the words out. "And… he died."

It was really hard to say the word, "died."

He was quiet. I think Mr. Freddrick was in shock. He thanked me for calling.

Two of Walt's daughters lived in the same apartment building. I couldn't reach either of them. I called their friend and told her.

"Holy hell, this is going to kill those girls. I'll find them and tell them."

I knew I could count on her.

Next, I called his daughter Robin who lived in Oregon. They were especially close.

She answered the phone. She had the kindest voice. My heart sunk.

I couldn't say it. I just couldn't do it.

I asked to speak to her husband.

She seemed to know something was terribly wrong. But she gave him the phone, and I told him, so that he could give her the news.

Next I needed to call his mother. She was a very sweet lady who I adored; she lived in Spokane, WA. Out of respect, I wanted her to hear the news from one of her daughters in person, rather than over the phone. I called my sister-in-law and let her know.

My parents were the last on my list, but I didn't want to call them. I just didn't.

Would they say, "I told you so?" I just couldn't hear that.

I called their house. Thank goodness my Mom's friend was over visiting her and she answered. I told her, and she said she would drive my mother over.

Word started to spread.

My cousin Bunkey called. She had just been visiting our family in Southern California and had returned to her home in New Jersey a couple days earlier.

"Lisa, do you want me to come back?"

"Yes," I said. "Please come back Bunkey."

--

People started coming over. Ryan was up from his nap and he was so happy with all the visitors - everyone was paying attention to him.

My friend, Angie, arrived with lots of food – her husband owned a Mexican restaurant.

She sat next to me and encouraged me to eat, in the way that you do for a 2-year-old.

"Take another bite, Lisa. Do it for Hannah, you need to eat for her. That's right, eat some more. Take one more bite."

I don't remember much else from that evening.

Except….. the same thought played over and over again in my mind: I hated myself for leaving the house when I did, and leaving him to die alone.

I kept saying, "Why did I leave the house? Why?"

There was no rationality at that point.

7

A MOTHER'S LOVE

If it was just that my parents had been worried about me, I could understand it.

But my father didn't like to lose, and so for him, Walt would always be the enemy. And I was complicit. He had stood strong in his conviction to shun me.

Walt never cared if they liked him or not. "Honey, I don't give a damn what they think about me, I just don't want you upset."

After we were married, I stopped going to holiday gatherings or events at their house.

It hurt. I somehow still wanted them to accept us.

When Ryan was born, my mother didn't even come to the hospital. They stood firm on the shunning.

Sometimes though, when Walt was at work or on a business trip, I would go see my mother. I convinced myself that it was OK to do that. My mother was a wonderful grandmother to her other grandchildren, and I wanted her to know my son.

She adored him.

During some of these visits I would run into my father. He basically kept up the silent treatment towards me, but he was never unkind to my son. In fact he would forget for a minute to be mean, and would smile and play with him.

Then he would quickly return to his grudge-holding self.

It was always awkward for me. And sad at the same time.

Walt knew I would go visit them at times. But eventually there came a time when he had had enough. Our son was still a baby, but he was now crawling and talking, and basically growing up into a little boy. Walt did not want Ryan to go anywhere if his father was not included. He did not want his son to grow up thinking this was normal or acceptable.

So I spent all holidays with my new little family, and no longer visited my mother.

At some point, my mother came to understand that if she wanted me in her life, she would have to bend.

When Ryan was about 1-year-old, my nephew was having a birthday party at a local park next to the beach. My mother agreed to attend, knowing that Walt would be there too. It had now been 8 years that we were together, and she was going to meet my husband for the very first time.

Walt wasn't the least bit nervous, but I knew my mother was.

When we arrived, we walked straight to my mother and I introduced them.

She gestured toward the water and said something like, "so we finally meet, by the shimmering sea." She was clearly uncomfortable, but she had shown up. Walt was very kind to her.

I was happy, because she was trying.

I knew it wasn't easy for her, and I also knew that she would have to face the wrath of my father for showing any kind of support towards my life choices.

My father did not attend the party, and continued not to budge on his stance.

--

After that, my mother attended all of the grandkids' parties and other events, even if Walt was present. They were always cordial to one another.

A year later, she even came to Ryan's birthday party at my house. She had never been to my home before. She was friendly and seemed comfortable being around Walt.

I can't remember how it came up, but someone said something about the non-acceptance by my parents towards our marriage.

Walt turned to my mother with a huge grin.

"You should be happy I took her off your hands!!"

And then he started laughing.

My God, how I loved that man.

8

THE DECISIONS

When someone dies, you very suddenly have to make all of these decisions about their service and their final resting place.

It's almost like a wedding:

Where will we have it?

What will I wear?

What will he wear?

Will we have music?

What food will we have afterwards?

The difference is that you have to do it all in a few days, instead of a few months. And you, and everyone around you, is crying and/or sad.

--

I had once read a woman's magazine article on the importance of knowing what your spouse would want if something were to happen to them.

One night I had asked Walt, "Honey, would you want to be buried or cremated?"

"Hell, honey! I don't care. Do whatever the hell you want to do with me. I won't know either way anyway." He had laughed.

So at least I knew that any decision I made would be fine.

Walt and I had gone to a funeral once where the embalmed person was in an open casket at the front of the church. He was definitely not a fan of someone being displayed in that way. I knew I would never do that.

I also did not plan on having a viewing. I didn't want to see him in a funeral home, propped up and not looking the way he had always looked.

His daughter, Robin, was on her way down from Oregon with her family. She called from a payphone.

"Lisa," she said, "Please don't do anything with Dad until I get there."

I knew she meant it was important to her to see him before any decision was made.

I decided to have a private viewing for Robin, and for his mother. I had learned this was important to her as well.

For me, I had already said goodbye.

—

My sisters barely left my side. Julie was artistic and created a program to hand out at the service. She looked through Walt's writings from a management course he had taken and added a quote of his:

"I now view dying as a final stage of growth in this life, and death as a curtain in front of what comes next. I believe the growth in me and what I am when I die, will carry over into the next life."

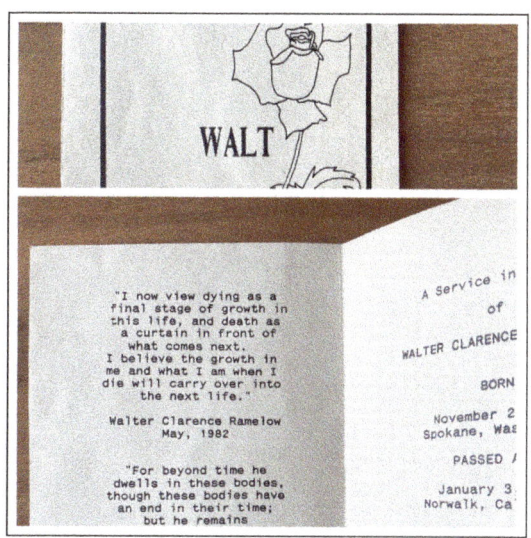

During all this funeral planning, someone told me that my father had offered to help me with the Rockwell benefits office in advising me on Walt's pension.

I wasn't sure. I just couldn't answer.

The last person I wanted to think about was my father.

--

There actually had been one small moment over the years when my father and Walt had briefly met.

My father had been an engineer at Rockwell during the Apollo days. One evening he came to an event at their Downey facility to celebrate a milestone in Space exploration. Walt was there too, and he and my father shook hands and introduced themselves. It was a positive interaction, but it was before my father knew about us.

If only he had just tried to accept Walt as a person.

--

"I just don't know," I would say when anyone mentioned my father wanting to come over and help me.

I wasn't sure if I wanted his help.

I continued the planning and decision-making that day, and finally went to sleep.

--

The next morning, there was a soft knock on my front door. I opened it.

My father was standing there.

9

STANDING ON MY PORCH

After Walt and I got married, I moved into his house, which was close to his work. I had now lived there for 5 years. My father had never been there.

That's why it startled me to see him when I opened the door.

He had his usual serious, stoic look on his face.

Fear gripped me. I could barely breathe just waiting for the meanness to come out, the "I told you this might happen" speech.

But he said nothing. We stared at each other for several seconds. I remained terrified.

And then, the strangest thing happened.

My father took a step forward and suddenly collapsed into my arms, sobbing like I had never seen him do before.

Men like my father did not cry; I had only seen him cry once in my entire life when my mother had been sick.

It felt so odd to be standing in my doorway now, comforting my father.

His grief for me was raw and palpable.

There was no "I told you so."

There was no "What are you going to do now?"

He made it clear that he would do whatever he could to help me.

I couldn't believe it.

We went to the Rockwell Benefits center together. I couldn't process much of what they were saying, so I was glad he was there.

--

As I look back now, I believe that my father's emotional breakdown that day was really him having to face the futility of his attitude over the last 10 years. He had to look at how much he had hurt me by holding back his love and acceptance.

From that day forward, he never said one unkind thing about Walt, or our marriage, or our relationship.

He treated me with almost a reverence, a deep respect for what had happened to me.

It took me awhile to get over my anger and resentment, but I did.

What good would it have done to hold onto it?

And my children needed grandparents.

I don't think my parents ever said they were sorry with words. But I knew they were.

They showed me everyday, by being the very best grandparents ever.

--

I love this photo.

My father was a very serious person, and he didn't smile in most pictures.

When Hannah was a month old, he nicknamed her "Ryan's squeaky sister" because she was always crying. He shortened it to "Squeak" and he called her that until he died.

This photo embodies how much he had changed towards me.

It was 2012; he was quite ill and in a wheelchair, but we somehow got him to Berkeley for Hannah's college graduation. He is proudly wearing a "Cal" jacket, and the look on his face is one of pure love for her. He can't help but smile.

He absolutely adored his Squeak, and he had been a wonderful grandfather to her and to Ryan.

--

He made it up to me.

10

LOSING IT

Some decisions were easy to make; some were not.

I listened to others' experiences of losing loved ones and tried to determine what to do.

A friend told me how when she finally found her birth mother, she learned she had already died, and there was no memorial or grave to visit. She found it very unsettling, and suggested it might be important to my children in the future to have somewhere they could go to remember their father.

I decided it might be better to bury him.

Walt's oldest daughter, Robin, would be arriving soon from Oregon with her family.

She was an old soul, as was he. Robin was a year old when Walt met and married her mother.

Being blood-related wasn't important to either of them; they understood each other, and he was 100% her father, except biologically.

--

Ryan was loving all the visitors that kept coming, but if he saw me looking sad, he became worried. He would cry and reach out to me for security.

When Robin and her family arrived, she and I went into my kids' bedroom and closed the door. I didn't want Ryan to see me sad, and I didn't know if I could hold it together much longer.

In her very kind sweet voice Robin said, "How are you doing, Lisa?"

It was in character for her to ask how I was doing, even though she had just lost her own father.

I then realized that I had held myself together since I had come home and found him on the kitchen floor. All that time I had kept in control, doing all the things that I needed to do.

But I looked at Robin, and said, "I don't know why he had to die."

I knew that, out of anyone, she would understand.

She put her arms around me, and that was it.

I was gone. I could not stop crying.

I then began screaming. "Why did he have to die?!?!" over and over again.

Robin held onto me, and handed me pillows to scream into, so that Ryan wouldn't hear me.

She put aside her own pain and let me grieve.

It was a kindness I will never forget.

--

The next day, Robin went with me to the cemetery. I chose Forest Lawn in Cypress, California.

The staff there was very kind. They put us in a big car and we drove from section to section. It reminded me of driving around with a real estate agent. They pointed things out and explained each area with pride and a smile.

After a couple hours, I was tiring of it and just wanted to make a decision.

Then we got to the section called "Compassion."

Walt was one of the most compassionate people I had ever met. I chose that one.

I picked a spot under a tree, so he would have shade.

I know that is not logical, but that is what happens when your mind is not operating correctly.

--

My beautiful stepdaughter, Robin, passed away unexpectedly in a tragic boating accident, in September, 2021. She had read all the stories of this memoir, and she was so incredibly supportive. She was the kindest soul I have ever met.

11

BUNKEY AND THE COFFEE POT

My mother, Rita, felt deeply sad for me, but she was driving me crazy. She had always been energetic, but now she was just plain frenetic.

Thank God for my cousin Bunkey. She had made it back from the east coast.

She knew how to handle my mother.

Every few minutes, my mother would wail about how horrible the situation was. That made Ryan anxious, and he would start crying. Bunkey would immediately start singing and dancing with him.

Next, my mother insisted that we had to serve coffee after the service.

This was the least of my concerns. I didn't care about coffee.

We put her in charge of bringing over her giant coffee pot that brewed 70 cups.

Also, my mother had firm ideas about funerals. She grew up in Philadelphia, and she went back there for every funeral. They were all similar: the viewing, the rosary, the mass, "Ave Maria," etc.

I wasn't doing any of that. Walt wasn't Catholic. He went along with our children being baptized because he knew I was doing it mostly to dress them up in little white outfits.

Plus, even though he was spiritual, he did not have favorable opinions towards church-type "rules."

Bunkey had attended many of those funerals with my mother. She reassured my mother, "Aunt Rita, don't worry. This is just what they call a 'California-style funeral.' That's how they do it out here."

If I hadn't been so sad at the time, I would have started laughing. She was so creative.

My mother seemed very worried that if I did it "wrong," then Walt might go to hell.

This irritated me, because she had wished he would go to hell many times while he was alive.

My mother even called her opera singer friend and handed me the phone so I could hear him sing.

Opera? I couldn't take it

Bunkey quickly took the phone and explained "Lisa doesn't want an opera singer. It doesn't go with a California funeral."

Then she cheerfully said, "Aunt Rita, how big is the coffee pot again? Are you sure we'll have enough?"

And my mother would talk again about how many cups it made.

I had to walk away.

I couldn't have done it without Bunkey.

I didn't hold any grudge towards my mother, I knew she was just so sad for her own little girl, me.

~ Rest in peace, Rita and Bunkey ~

12

THE LONG WALK

I had arranged for a private viewing for Robin and Walt's mother.

I picked out jeans and a comfortable flannel shirt for him to wear, the kind he wore on the weekends.

I originally had no intention of going, but some people had told me that it was a comforting experience. I decided I would go along to the mortuary, and make up my mind about seeing him once I got there.

--

My mother and Bunkey were quite used to viewings; they had been to many.

They went in together.

When they came out, Bunkey said, "Lisa he looks great!"

But my mother started wailing, "Don't go in there! He looks just terrible!"

I became very upset.

What was terrible about him? Did they not put the right clothes on him? Did they not put the things in his pockets that I had given them?

I looked at Bunkey and my mother, and I didn't know whom to believe.

Teresa stood up. "Lisa, I'll go."

She knew that she was the only one I would believe. This was a really big sacrifice for her. I don't think she had ever seen a dead body before, and she had not planned on it. But she did it for me.

It was a kindness I will never forget.

She disappeared for a minute and then returned.

She spoke quietly. "They did everything that you asked them to do. His hair looks a little different, but not in a way that will bother you."

She said she would go in with me.

I stood at the door and could see him up at the front of the room.

Robin was standing over him with her husband at her side. I was in awe of her strength. She spoke quietly and calmly. "Dad, thank you for accepting me as your daughter. Thank you for loving me the way you did."

They left the room. Now it was my turn.

He was probably 10 feet from the door. But I think it took 20 minutes for me to reach him.

Teresa stayed by my side and held me up. I don't know why this was such a different experience than the emergency room.

My entire body trembled; I couldn't stop it. With each step my foot shook and I felt like I was going to fall over. Teresa said nothing but kept a tight grip on me, and when we got there, she didn't let go.

I stood and looked at him. He looked nice.

I was afraid to touch him; I wanted to remember how warm and real he had felt in the hospital.

I had the 2 little photos of our children with me.

I put them on his chest.

I had already said goodbye in the emergency room, but this seemed even more real.

He was never coming back.

My Walt was gone.

13

THE BABY WAS HUNGRY

The funeral was to be held at an on-site chapel at the cemetery.

I wanted both of my children to be there. This was one of the easy decisions. It didn't matter to me whether they would remember it or not, I wanted them to always know they were there to say goodbye to their father.

And I knew that's what Walt would want.

I wasn't having an open casket, so I didn't have to worry about Ryan being confused.

But I did have a few concerns about how the kids would hold up during an hour-long service. I didn't know if Ryan would get antsy and want to run around. Hannah was usually a fussy baby, so I was worried that she might need extra attention – I didn't want to have to go outside and walk around with her.

I wanted my attention to be fully on the service honoring Walt, I wanted to experience every second of it.

I decided to put in some contingency plans in case things didn't go well with the kids.

--

I had a close friend, Angie, who I had known since grade school.

We had become reacquainted as Moms because we had similar circumstances: her son was close to Ryan's age, and she had twin boys a couple months older than Hannah. We both had husbands who worked a lot of hours.

We talked on the phone every day about mundane things like laundry and how our kids had slept. We both greatly appreciated our lives, but it was nice to have someone to vent to each day. I could tell Angie anything. She didn't mind hearing how tired I was, or how frustrated I might be. And I liked hearing her daily stories as well. We would always end up laughing.

Angie had come over that first night, but she respectfully stayed in the background while my family stepped in to help me make arrangements.

I did have a big favor to ask of her though.

I called and we discussed it. She said yes right away.

--

The day of the funeral arrived.

It wasn't easy for Angie to arrange for a babysitter for her babies and their brother, but her mother and sister agreed to do it.

She arrived early at the chapel, waiting quietly in the back in case I needed her.

Walt's daughters sat with me, Ryan, and Hannah in the front row, and my sisters and brother were behind me.

The service began with an officiate from the cemetery.

Within a few minutes, the baby became fussy. I could not calm her down. She kept wiggling around and whimpering. Ryan whispered, "Mommy, Hannah's crying."

Finally, I turned to my sister and said, "Go get Angie."

Angie walked quietly up the aisle, and I handed Hannah to her. She took her to the back and within a minute, I no longer heard her crying.

A few minutes later, Angie walked back up the aisle and handed me a happy baby.

I smiled at her and nodded.

It was my silent way of thanking her, for nursing my baby girl.

It was, again, a kindness I will never forget.

14

DR. JEKYLL AND MR. RAMELOW

The funeral chapel was overflowing.

Walt had worked as a Project Manager at Rockwell. He tended to hire "misfits," those people who couldn't be hired elsewhere. He saw past whatever held them back, and could tell they had something to offer if given a chance.

Once someone was hired, they were very loyal to him.

I remember a smart young man who only had a "C" average from college and couldn't get a job. Walt learned that his upbringing had been very difficult. He looked past his GPA and hired him. That young man worked so hard.

I also remember a man who always wore a sailor hat and a tan jacket. He ran up and down the aisles carrying these large data tapes. He never looked up, or said anything to anyone, but he was great at his job.

Then there was Ed. When he was first hired, he worked on a proposal with two other engineers. Walt listened to their entire proposal without saying a word. He waited until they were finished, and then he looked at them and said, "You ain't got shit!"

Ed had been horrified at how blunt he was, and wasn't sure he wanted to work with him.

But he stayed, and after time, Ed grew to appreciate Walt. He even presented him with this plaque with his quote on it. I don't think I ever saw Walt so delighted with any present he had ever received – he loved it.

All of these people came.

--

Our friend, Adele, was the first speaker. She said, "Walt had confidence in people, more than they had in themselves."

When it was Ed's turn he began his funeral speech with, "I didn't like him at first. In fact, Walt did not make a good first, second, or third impression."

Everyone laughed.

My favorite part was when he said that Walt was a "Dr. Jekyll and Mr. Ramelow," describing his quiet, reflective side versus his bad-boy side.

Walt would have loved it.

Ed concluded with, "Aside from leaving his family, I am certain that Walt died with no regrets."

I agreed.

15

WISE MEN SAY

I carefully chose the music for Walt's service.

--

Every morning when Walt left for work, he bent down to hug Ryan goodbye and he always said, "See you later, Alligator!"

It was a line from a popular song of the 50's. It would be a really unconventional song choice for a funeral, but that's what I wanted. I chose it for early in the service.

I wanted one more song.

Walt had grown up in the 50's, and Elvis Presley was a big part of his generation. I remembered the New Year's Eve when Ryan was 1½ and Walt had put on Elvis' greatest hits. Ryan stood on our coffee table and danced, while Walt danced around the table next to him.

I did not grow up with Elvis' music, but I had always really liked one of his songs. It was slow and melodic, and told a love story of two people that didn't really belong together, and yet were somehow drawn to each other.

This resonated with me, because it was exactly my experience; it was what had happened to me in loving Walt. I didn't want to fall in love with him because he was older than me. But I couldn't help it.

"Would it be a sin, if I can't help, falling in love with you."

I knew it would be perfect to honor Walt, to describe how we loved each other.

At the end of the service, the song began: "Wise men say, only fools rush in, But I can't help, falling in love with you."

I remember every second, every note.

Time stood still. It made an imprint on my heart, my psyche, on my soul - every part of me.

--

After the service, we went to the gravesite for the burial. I had a small ivory heart-shaped pillow with a banner that said "Daddy" in gold letters. I gave it to Ryan to put on top of the casket before it was lowered into the ground. He didn't really understand what was happening, but he was happy to run over and place it there.

We returned to our home, and many people came to show their respects.

There was plenty of coffee for everyone. That made my mother happy.

In the days that followed, I threw away the clothes I had worn to his funeral: a cream-colored blouse and a flowered skirt. I had chosen those over the traditional black, because I felt it was more celebratory, and I looked at his memorial service as a celebration of his life.

But I never wanted to wear those clothes again.

I also gave away the 2-piece sweat suit outfit I was wearing when I found him on the kitchen floor. My sister had given it to me for Christmas. But when I looked at it, all I could think of was that day: the moment when I found him, the pacing in the waiting room, saying goodbye, looking at his blue eyes for the last time.

I could never wear that again either. I donated it to charity.

--

Years later I found these photos that were taken on that day. I didn't remember them being taken.

I originally did not like this first picture, because I am smiling. I don't know why I smiled, probably because someone held up a camera.

I can appreciate it now though, because it has all 5 of Walt's children together.

I don't remember this other one being taken either, of me nursing Hannah on that day. But it is a reminder of how young I was, and how much responsibility I had ahead of me.

--

Walt's funeral song has continued to have an effect on me for many years.

When you lose someone, you can give away the clothes you wear. You can give away your loved one's clothes too. You can even move somewhere else.

But….. the song you played at such a momentous occasion will always be out there for you to hear again. Someday, somewhere, it will begin playing. It might be at a celebration, or it may turn up in a movie you are watching.

It will have a big impact on you when you suddenly hear those first few notes.

I remember the first time this happened to me. It was a few years after Walt's death and I was attending a wedding. Towards the end of the service, the Elvis Presley song began. I hadn't been expecting it – the couple was young, from a different generation than Elvis. I didn't know it was coming.

An explosion of emotion overcame me, and I quickly got up and left the church. I didn't want to feel sorry for myself, but I did. I walked outside in the dark for a long time.

It had such a profound and visceral effect on me.

Even now, after many years, it still has this impact.

I no longer get upset; it's different now.

When I hear Walt's funeral song, I need the world to stop for just those few minutes.

The first few very melodic notes begin and I feel frozen.

I need to stop time.

I need to tune out everything happening around me.

I cannot hear people.

I cannot talk to people.

Every cell in my body has to absorb every note, so I can give gratitude to the man who gave me so much.

I close my eyes for those 3 minutes and go into a different place.

I can always listen to it. But all around me, time must stand still.

That is the only way.

"Some things are meant to be."

"Take my hand. Take my whole life too."

I couldn't help falling in love with you honey.

16

SWEET LAUGHTER

Everything was over.

The funeral was done.

Everyone who was visiting from far away had gone home. People returned to their jobs and resumed their lives. It was all, sort of, "over."

My sister Teresa, and her baby, Rachel, decided to stay with us for the next 2 weeks. This was incredibly helpful to me. I was very grateful for the company. I could put off facing what I knew would be a very difficult time.

--

Having them there also made it easier for me with Ryan. He was used to having his routine changed up every other week, because Walt had traveled quite a bit for his job.

Walt worked one week at home, and then the following week he would travel to Kennedy Space Center in Florida. He would leave on Monday and come back late Friday.

Each week he was gone, Ryan knew, "Oh! Daddy's on his trip!"

Having Teresa and Rachel with us seemed to distract Ryan – I think he just figured "Daddy's on a trip."

During those 2 weeks, we just played with the kids, went on walks, and pretended that everything was normal, even though it wasn't.

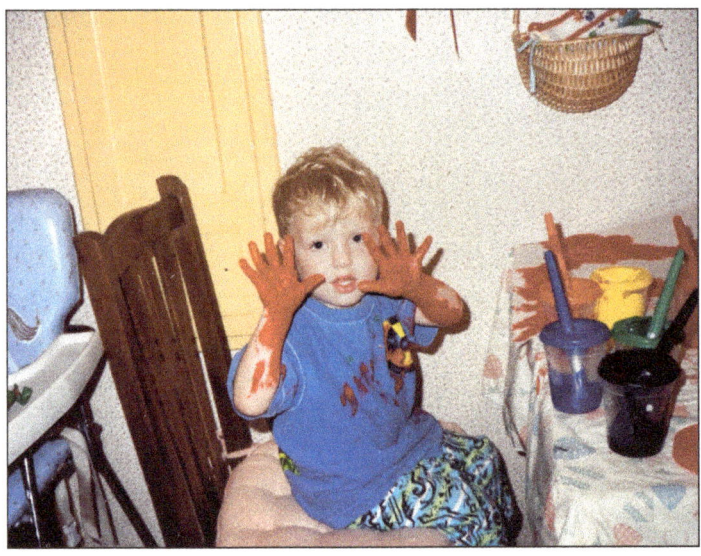

I let Ryan pretty much do whatever he wanted. He watched a lot of Disney movies, and he was delighted to have his fun aunt there, along with his cousin Rachel.

The babies liked sitting in this new swing I had gotten; we put them in there every day and played fun music.

This was the beginning of my "pretending he didn't really die" stage. But I needed this time. I needed to pretend a little longer.

At some point during those two weeks, we all got sick with a cold.

Both of the babies were congested and not sleeping well. I ran to the store and purchased a bottle of infant decongestant for each of them. We followed the directions and gave it to them every 4 hours, hoping they would sleep better.

The problem was we were also congested, and quite miserable. But we were both nursing our babies and didn't want to take any medication.

After a couple days, neither of us had gotten much sleep, and both the babies were cranky. We were exhausted. I called my pediatrician's office and explained the situation. I asked, "Well, if we're giving the babies this medicine, then can't we take it too?"

The doctor answered, "No. You shouldn't take it if you're breastfeeding."

I hung up and turned to Teresa, "They said we shouldn't take anything."

Teresa didn't care what they had said. She picked up Rachel's bottle of medicine, unscrewed the top, and took out the dropper.

"I don't care," she said. "If I can give it to Rach, then I can take it too."

And then, she proceeded to guzzle the entire bottle of infant decongestant.

I looked at her and thought, "she's right. That makes sense!" and I quickly did the same. I opened Hannah's bottle, and drank hers too.

We were both laughing.

--

At one point during those 2 weeks, Teresa had both of the girls on her lap in the kitchen. Her daughter Rachel was holding some keys, and she was shaking them around.

Hannah wasn't really looking at anything in particular. But she just started wildly laughing whenever Rachel shook the keys.

I think that was the first time I had ever heard her laugh. She was not even a particularly "smiley" baby; she had smiled the most for her father when he got home from work everyday and picked her up.

It was so unusual, that I ran to get my video camera and capture it. Hannah continued to laugh, but she never looked over at her cousin Rachel who was shaking the keys, nor at her brother who was busy dancing right there in the kitchen. She was staring to the side, to nothing it seemed in particular.

I always felt like maybe her father was present right there with us in the kitchen, and it was he who she was staring at, and the reason she was laughing with such delight.

I didn't pick up the camera again for several months. But I was happy I had this small amount of video as a reminder of those 2 weeks. This is a screenshot from the video.

17

PRETENDING

Eventually Teresa and Rachel went home.

Now, everyone was gone. They all returned to their lives, as they should.

Because, it was all over, right?

Intellectually, I understood this. People had to live their own lives. My tragedy was not their tragedy.

But it was a hollow, empty, and lonely type of existence.

Now the real pain of adjustment was beginning.

Everyday, I woke up knowing that my life was forever different. It was like a smack in the face every morning.

--

The early mornings were so very strange for me. There were no sounds of Walt getting ready. I couldn't hear him go outside, I didn't hear him shaving, I didn't hear the refrigerator opening and closing.

I lay there and unconsciously began a routine.

I was letting Ryan sleep in my bed every night, and when he woke up I let him jump and play on the bed. I would get Hannah out of her crib, but instead of heading to our family room to nurse her, I stayed in the bedroom.

I watched the clock.

Once it got to 9 AM, I could start my pretending.

I would tell Ryan, "let's get up and have breakfast!" and the 3 of us would head to the kitchen.

I put Hannah in her baby carrier, and made them breakfast. I could pretend that everything was normal.

It was after 9AM, right? So Walt would be at work, right?

I got the kids dressed, I did household chores, and we went out in the backyard for a while.

The world was the same, right?

I knew it wasn't.

I was pretending.

I had to, in order to keep my sanity. I didn't even know I was doing it.

I didn't lie to Ryan and pretend "out loud" that his father was alive. It was just something I was doing in my head.

On one of those mornings, I thought, "Hmmm, I wonder what would happen if I called Walt's work number."

Rockwell had some type of answering system set up, and they hadn't yet changed it since he died.

So that morning, I called his number: 92*-2207. I reached the familiar message: "Hello. This is Walt Ramelow ……"

It was so good to hear his voice! I loved it. It made me so happy.

"Hmmm," I would say to myself. "He's busy."

I knew he wasn't busy. But I needed to tell myself that.

And then, Voice #2 would chime in: "No, he's not busy, you know he died."

I didn't like Voice #2.

Voice #1 would override Voice #2 and say, "Whatever! Just be quiet!"

Thirty minutes later, I would call his number again: 92*-2207.

I would hear his voice again saying that he could not come to the phone.

"Hmmm," I would tell myself. "I guess he's still busy."

Voice #2 spoke up again: "What is wrong with you? Why are you doing this?"

Voice #1 did not want to hear Voice #2: "Be quiet, I can do what I want!"

I did this every single day. I was compelled to do it.

Besides calling his work phone number, I did other things to pretend that he had not died.

There were messages from Walt on my answering machine that I hadn't erased. He had left them when he was traveling on his business trips.

I would hit the rewind button many times during the day to hear him say, "Hi honey. I'm calling to say good night. Take care of yourself and the baby."

I loved hearing his voice.

I played them over and over, way too much, obsessively.

Then, lunchtime would come. Walt would generally call and see what we were up to, and ask if I needed anything at the store that he could pick up on his way home.

But, he didn't call.

So what did I do? I called him.

92*-2207

"Oh," I would tell myself. "He's still busy."

Voice #2: "You know he's not busy."

"Shut-up!" I would yell at Voice #2.

Eventually the mailman would come, and Ryan would do his usual running to the door saying, "Daddy's home!"

I would always tell him the truth, that Daddy could never come home again. That Daddy did not want to leave us and would come home if he could. Ryan would ask the same questions everyday, "Can we go see Daddy in the car? Can we go see Daddy on a plane?" It was always the same.

Every time, I would start crying again, and waves of despair would wash over me. I would sit on the couch crying, and then Ryan would get upset and say, "Mommy, why are you crying again?"

There was no way to explain Walt's death, nor the depth of my sadness. I had to try so hard every afternoon to "cheer up" and be the mother my kids needed me to be. I knew it wasn't healthy for them to see me crying every day.

--

Everywhere I went, on even the smallest errands, people understandably continued to live their lives. They seemed happy and were smiling, and it somehow frustrated me. I wanted to scream at them, "Why are you all so happy? Don't you know that Walt died?!"

I knew all these people didn't even know Walt, and this made no sense at all.

But I needed to be in this land of make-believe.

One time I went out to buy more Aquaphor that the doctor had recommended for Hannah's dry skin. Walt had bought it before; I checked the price tag, it was from Fedco.

Walt LOVED Fedco. I did not.

But I headed to Fedco and put the kids in a cart. I found the skin care section and saw the Aquaphor. I stood there in front of a shelf full of Aquaphor and started bawling. I kept picturing him standing in that exact spot. I couldn't move.

People passed by me and I wondered what they were thinking, but I couldn't stop crying.

A lady stopped and asked me if I needed something, and I said between sobs, "I found the Aquaphor."

It made no sense to her, but she was very kind.

--

I returned home. And what did I do?

I called 92*-2207.

--

Each day I descended further into a very dark place. On some level I was aware of this, but I was not yet ready to face it.

18

RE-ENACTING

I kept thinking, "Why did he have to die?"

But, truly, I already knew how and why.

How: He died from a heart attack.

Why: Probably because he had smoked since he was a teenager.

--

Ugh. I hated that he smoked. I knew about it from the moment I met him. But I somehow convinced myself that it would be OK, and he would one day quit.

We argued about it for years, we even broke up over it a few times when we were dating. He quit a few times, but he always started up again.

When we decided to get married, he promised he would try again once we were married. He never stopped. Finally I just decided to quit badgering him about it.

And we had an agreement: he only smoked outside with the door closed. And not around the kids.

--

So, I knew how, and I knew why. And yet, I couldn't stay focused on these concrete facts for very long.

I was operating on an emotional plane. There was not much room in my brain for logic.

I didn't want to look at these realities because it meant I would be blaming him for not taking better care of himself. And I just couldn't bear to have a negative thought about him. I felt so sorry for him and all that he would be missing.

Instead, I continued to blame myself.

I had a new obsession: asking myself over and over again, "Why did I leave the house when I did on the day he died? Maybe if I had stayed home, I could have gotten him help sooner and he would have lived."

I also focused my attention on how I now hated my kitchen floor. Honestly, I never really liked that floor.

--

Walt's house was what I would call "50's-guy-chic," with brown wood paneling, brown carpet, and an ugly linoleum kitchen floor. When we got married, I moved there because it was close to his work, and I planned to quit my job once we had a baby.

I did try to put my own touches everywhere, adding wallpaper and bringing out whatever pretty colors that I could.

--

When I found him on the floor, he had an unlit cigarette on his chest. That meant he was probably holding it and about to head outside. But how did it land where it did, and what exactly had happened?

I would never know, because I had left the house. And that was what I was now focused on.

--

Every night, in the middle of the night, I fed the baby.

After she went back to sleep, I would go into the kitchen, usually around 3 or 4AM. I would stand where Walt had fallen. I would actually try to "fall" and see if I could land the same way he had.

I would lie on the floor where he had been.

Why was he on his back? If someone had a heart attack, wouldn't they slump forward?

I lay there on my kitchen floor contemplating what had happened to him. My questions continued. Did he lie down, knowing something was wrong, and call my name? Could I have saved him?

Oh dear! I should not have left the house! Maybe if I had stayed, then he would have lived.

That's why he was dead. Because I left the house.

And then he died on this hideous floor.

I repeated this scenario almost every night, trying somehow to come up with an answer, and to absolve myself of my nagging guilt.

Eventually, I would go back to bed, and try to sleep for an hour or two before the kids woke up.

Then I would wait until it was safely past 9AM, and pick up the phone.

And dial 92*-2207

--

Photo: I can't believe I found this photo - Hannah is standing exactly where he died. It doesn't upset me, because she is so cute.

19

THE BOOK, "WIDOWED"

My friend Angie became my lifeline.

It was too hard to get together with 3 babies and 2 toddlers, so we talked on the phone everyday. She would ask me how I slept, how the baby was, and how Ryan had been with the mailman the day before.

I don't know how many times she had to hear me talk about my theory that if I hadn't left the house, Walt would magically still be alive.

One day she came over and gave me a book she thought would help; it was called, "Widowed."

I read the first couple chapters. The author had lost her husband when her children were 3 and 5. But his death had affected her very differently than what I was experiencing. She believed that since God took her husband, he would never take her kids. So she was at peace about that.

I could not have been more opposite.

My constant refrain was, "If God was that much of an asshole to take my husband, then he's going to come take my kids too."

I was constantly fearful that something else bad was going to happen.

I didn't leave the house very much.

The kids had slept in the room next to ours. But I was too afraid to have them away from me. I took Hannah's crib apart and rebuilt it in my bedroom, and Ryan slept in the bed with me. I went to a hardware store and got a sliding bolt and put it on the bedroom door, so we were all locked in together every night.

I was already torturing myself with guilt, and now I expanded it further.

I remembered the exact day when I had finally stopped worrying that something might happen to Walt. He had always been patient with me about this, but one night he had said, "Honey! Stop worrying, I'm not going to die on you!"

Soon after, I finally let go of that worry.

The memory of letting go of that fear was so crystal clear to me. I was driving on the 405 freeway with my kids and I thought, "It's time to stop worrying about this. We have an adorable little boy and a sweet new baby girl. This is ridiculous."

Walt was right, it did no good to worry. I let it go.

I felt so relieved. I took a deep breath and felt so free.

--

Three weeks later, he was dead.

This was the basis for my new guilt.

Oh no! What had I done?

I should never have stopped worrying about him. Why did I do that?

And why did I leave the house and leave him to die alone?

Now my kids wouldn't have a father.

And it was all because of me.

Somewhere deep down, I knew this was not logical. And yet I continued on this path, not able to stop myself from having these thoughts.

--

Angie knew I was not well.

Without mentioning it, she started calling local hospitals trying to find a grief support group for me to attend.

She knew I was going down a dark deep hole. Fast.

20

THE GRIEF GROUP

During my daily call to Angie, she said, "Lisa, would you consider going to a support group?"

"Maybe," I said, "but I wouldn't know how to find one."

Then she told me very sweetly how she had already done that for me.

--

The group met on Wednesdays in a building near the traffic circle in Long Beach.

The first time I went, I sat in the back and silently wept.

There was only one man in the group, the rest women, most of them older than me. Some had been coming over 5 years. I found that strange, and rather discouraging.

There was a range of experiences in the group. One lady was already dating just 3 months after her husband died. I tried not to judge her, but I would have felt like I was cheating if I did that.

I liked a lady named Barbara. She also lost her husband suddenly. He was out walking the dog, had a heart attack, and died instantly on someone's lawn. Barbara and I bonded over one of the worst things about a sudden death: you don't get to say goodbye.

The other people in the group had spouses with long illnesses. We knew we were lucky we did not have to watch our husbands go through pain and medical treatments, and face the uncertainty of their future.

Our pain was somewhat different.

One evening, a lady shared that her husband had been sick for 7 months before he died, and she lamented that it was not enough time to say goodbye.

Barbara and I glanced at each other. We knew we were thinking the same thing: we would have been happy with 7 minutes, or even 7 seconds, to say goodbye.

Not being able to say goodbye is a special kind of torture. You relive every "last" moment you had with the person.

I was so happy that Walt and I had made up that morning of his death. I don't know how I could have handled it if we hadn't.

I also felt grateful that he had lived to meet our daughter, Hannah. I knew she would never remember him, but it was so important to me that she knew her father had loved her, held her, and spoken to her. And I had pictures of them together.

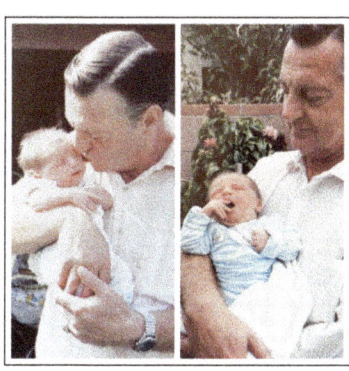

The women in the group shared a lot about the loneliness they felt, how difficult it was to be in an empty house every night.

They kept telling me I was lucky that I had my kids, that I had someone around every evening. That was true, but I felt absolutely exhausted.

I didn't feel lucky.

Then, one week, a new person joined the group. Her husband had died when she was 6 months pregnant.

Her husband had never met their baby.

I took a deep breath.

NOW.... I was lucky.

21

ANGER? NOT ME

One phase of the grieving process is "Anger."

But, I wasn't angry. Not at all. My overwhelming emotion was of sadness for Walt. He had been so happy being a father again.

--

When I was pregnant, Walt warned me that it would be a girl. He said, "I only make girls," and he would smile.

He said he didn't feel the need to have a son, the way some men did.

In the delivery room, he was quiet and, I think, shocked, when the doctor said it was a boy.

Even more than that, Ryan was a clone of Walt, with his turquoise blue eyes. Even the nurses commented there was no mistaking who the father of this baby was.

When Ryan was a couple months old, Walt became very reflective one evening. He told me he now finally understood why having a son meant so much to many men. I think this revelation rather surprised him. He was happy that the name "Ryan" meant "The Little King."

So instead of anger, I felt an overwhelming feeling of sadness for all that Walt was going to miss.

One night after he died, both kids woke up at around 3 AM. I sat on the floor changing the baby; she wouldn't stop crying. Ryan woke up and sat next to me crying too.

Beyond exhausted, I felt frantic. I thought I was going to lose my mind. I couldn't calm either of them down. I did not know how I could go on.

A 5x7 photo of Walt sat high on a shelf. I happened to look up at it during all the crying.

In my mind, it looked like he was talking to me. I thought he was saying, "Now, honey, try to be a little more patient with the kids."

"SHUT UP!!!" I yelled at the photo.

"Just SHUT UP!!! You left me with this mess!! You said you wouldn't leave me! You told me not to worry! You said you wouldn't die! And you did! You left me to do this all by myself!!"

The kids now screamed even louder. I was surprised the neighbors did not call the police.

I put the kids in my bed and bolted the bedroom door. I got in next to them, and lay there listening to them crying, wondering if I would ever be OK again.

--

The next morning I went to Walt's photo and told him I was sorry.

I knew I needed more help.

22

I NEED A TEENAGER

I knew if I didn't get some help, I would not be able to fulfill the promise I made to Walt in the emergency room, that I would take care of our children.

Walt and I did not have any babysitters. We loved being with our kids, and he worked so much that when he was home, he didn't want to go out. He loved gardening and barbequing, and just being home all day on the weekends.

--

That next morning after I had screamed at his picture, I got my kids ready, put them in the double stroller, and walked the few blocks to the local high school.

I went into the front office.

They led me to the principal, and I explained that I wanted to hire a teenager who could come over and help me. They had a student newspaper, and he said he would put an ad in for me.

I don't remember the principal's name, but he showed so much empathy and true sorrow for my situation.

It was another kindness I will never forget, from a wonderful stranger.

--

The first teenager I hired was George.

George loved playing ball with Ryan out in the yard. They ran all over the place as if they were the same age. That was great, except he had no interest in Hannah, and I needed someone who could watch both of them.

Next I hired Estella; she was perfect!

She thought of Hannah as her own little dolly. And she adored Ryan. She had so much patience. Toddlers like to repeat the same thing 100 times, and she never tired of anything he did.

When she first began coming over, I would not leave the room. I was too afraid. I didn't trust anyone.

Eventually, I gained enough courage to leave her alone with them, and I went to my room and closed the door. Mostly, I just needed to cry alone; if I cried too much around the kids, they became upset.

Finally, one day while Estella watched the kids, I allowed myself to fall asleep.

I woke up in a panic, overwhelmed with fear, forgetting for a moment where the kids were. I then quickly remembered I had left them with Estella, but I ran to the family room to make sure they were OK.

Of course they were. Estella had Hannah in her walker and was handing her toys to play with, while Ryan was dancing to some music she had quietly playing.

The kids loved being with Estella, and eventually with her help, I felt some relief.

My mind was getting a little better each day with a little extra rest, and with time to grieve in private.

23

THE DREAMS

Even though I felt a little better during the day, the nights continued to haunt me.

It was because of The Dreams.

I had heard of people having happy dream visits from their loved ones who had passed.

It wasn't like that for me. My subconscious mind refused to believe what my conscious mind was telling it. They fought it out every night in the same basic dream. Sometimes it varied, but it always ended the same.

Walt would come to me. He was alive.

I would ask him, "How are you here? You died! On the kitchen floor, when I left the house."

"No," he would say. "Honey, I didn't die, I'm right here."

I would argue with him and use logic.

"I'm sure you died. We had a service. Everyone from Rockwell was there. My mother brought her coffee pot."

He would tell me over and over, "Honey, you're wrong. I'm alive. I didn't go anywhere."

"But you were on the kitchen floor. I saw them put your coffin in the ground."

He would answer, "No, you just dreamt that. This is what's real. I didn't die. I'm right here."

The conversation would go back and forth, as I questioned him and what I remembered. But he was always SO convincing.

Finally, I would believe him.

HE WAS ALIVE!

It had all just been a terrible dream!

Once I was convinced that he was actually alive, and ONLY THEN….

I would wake up.

It was pure torture.

My heart sank each time.

Oh. He's not alive. He's dead.

It's true.

He is gone.

I was so mad at my brain. "Stop it stupid brain! Just STOP it already!!"

--

Years later……

I would sometimes have a different version of the dream.

Walt would appear. He did not try to convince me that he hadn't died. Instead, he always had an explanation for being gone. Usually he told me he was working on a top-secret project, and he couldn't tell me about it.

I would question him of course.

I would always be mad that he had left and hadn't told me, but that was OK, because… REJOICE!!!

He was going to see our children! I was SO excited for him to meet Ryan and Hannah all grown up. I told him how wonderful they were, that he would be so proud of how they had turned out.

I had tried my best.

Without saying a word, he would just quietly smile at me.

And then…

I would wake up.

Sigh. It wasn't true.

He would never, ever, meet grown-up Ryan and Hannah.

He would never know these two people that he had loved so very much.

My heart always hurt; he had missed everything.

But I no longer got mad at myself.

24

SLOW DANCING ON HIS GRAVE

I had Walt buried in a cemetery not far from our house. I wanted Ryan and Hannah to have a place they could go to honor and remember their father.

I began taking the kids there to visit not long after Walt's death.

I mostly liked going on an ordinary weekday when few people were there; I liked the privacy of being alone with him.

--

Walt's grave was far away from the street. Once Hannah started walking, I knew I could let the kids run around and I didn't have to worry. I did have to remind them not to take things off the other graves – there were lots of those pinwheels they loved.

Every time, I brought a portable cassette player with me, along with a tape of Walt's funeral music.

I also brought recent photos of the kids similar to the ones I had laid on his chest. I taped them to his tombstone. I wanted him to somehow "see" how they were growing up. It gave me comfort.

While the kids played, I sat and talked to him.

Then, I'd lie face down on his grave, approximating where his body was. I would close my eyes, turn my head, and rest my cheek on the grass. I felt like I was lying on top of him. I imagined him reaching up and putting his arms around me, telling me that everything would be OK.

After that, I stood up and turned on the tape recorder.

I stood on his grave, and crossed my arms across my chest. His funeral song would start... "Wise men say..."

I would turn very slowly around, one step at a time, moving my hands lovingly up and down each of my arms, pretending he was there dancing with me.

It was the one place I could really feel his presence.

--

When the song ended, I told him goodbye.

Then, I called for the kids to come back.

If they had taken anything off a grave, I tried to put it all back in the correct place.

If I got it wrong, I felt like all the souls there were very forgiving.

--

One year on Father's Day I was planning to head to the cemetery with the kids. My brother-in-law, my children's uncle, came by and suggested that I let him take them to the park instead, along with his two kids, their cousins.

I stopped to think about it, and in that moment I realized my children were better off spending time with a real-life man, than going with me to his grave.

I said yes.

I had to move forward, it was the only way to get better.

--

My favorite photos are of Hannah running all over, with Ryan trying to get her to come back.

25

THE WIDOW CARD

A few months after Walt died, my tax return check came. It was addressed to "Mr. & Mrs. Walt Ramelow."

I went to the bank to deposit it. The teller would not accept it without Walt's signature. I couldn't then just sign his name and hand it back to her.

My mother was waiting in the car with the kids. She said, "Go back in there and tell them you're a widow."

I was sort of horrified, and did not want to do that.

I went back and got a different teller. I explained that he had died. She said she couldn't take the check without his signature. Or I needed to bring in a death certificate. Really?

I was frustrated. I felt like saying, "Well, do you want me to dig him up and have him sign it?"

But I didn't say that.

--

When you become widowed, there are so many things to deal with beyond the obvious grieving.

There will come a time when you need to fill out a form, maybe in a doctor's office, and you will have to check a box regarding your marital status.

There it is, that little empty box next to the word, "Widowed".

It stops you in your tracks for a moment. It's just another way for reality to smack you in the face. You hold the pen and take a deep breath, and then you put down an "X" in that little box. It's true now. You are a widow. There is no going back.

Then there are the school forms you need to fill out for your kids. They ask for "Mother's name."

That one is easy.

Then, "Father's name."

Uh-oh. You pause.

Do you write his name?

Do you write, "Deceased"?

Do you just draw a line through the question?

You make a choice. But whatever you choose, there it is again. You are a widow, and your children do not have a father.

--

There were times over the years that I could hear my mother's voice saying, "Tell them you're a widow."

I understood that she wanted people to be more sympathetic to me. But somehow it always felt wrong to me to do that. It felt like I was asking for something extra, and perhaps it was just a declaration that I did not want to keep making. After all, I had to wake up to it every single day.

I didn't want special favors.

Focusing on it also made me feel like I was living in non-acceptance.

And being a widow was now part of my being. I didn't need to declare it to anyone.

26

DEATH VS. DIVORCE

My best friend at Rockwell was Robin H. (this is a different Robin than Walt's daughter).

Walt had been Robin H.'s first boss right out of college.

We both happened to get married the same year, and then we had babies within one day of each other.

The night of Walt's death, Robin H. had heard the news and had come right over. She was there that whole first evening.

Later in that year, Robin H. was getting a divorce. She had joined a divorce support group to help her adjust to her new situation.

One day we were chatting about our different groups.

Listening to Robin H.'s divorce group experience allowed me to have some gratitude for my own situation, even though it was difficult. There were things that the divorced women had to deal with that I did not have to.

I did not have to deal with custody issues as those ladies did. My kids would always be with me.

I did not have the big decision of whether or not to get a divorce.

Becoming a widow just happened to me; I didn't have to spend hours pondering what I should do, there was no decision.

More importantly, Robin H. said that everyone in her group thought their husband was a terrible person with not one redeeming quality. Hmmmm.

That was so different from what was happening in my Grief support group. In my group, many of the women talked about their husbands as if they were saints and had never done anything wrong.

This dichotomy started up my thinking.

I knew that neither of these depictions was correct. The husbands who had died were certainly not perfect. The divorced group's husbands could not have been totally bad, right?

I wondered if the women in the divorce group would be better off if they allowed themselves to recognize something good about their spouses. It didn't seem wise to hold on to such resentment.

And I wondered if a similar principle applied in the Grief Group.

Maybe it would be helpful to recognize that our deceased loved ones were not perfect.

I had noticed the women who had been in the Grief Group the longest, were the ones who could only say nice things about their husbands.

And I realized I liked hearing from the women who spoke up and admitted there were things about their husbands they did not miss. It was honestly refreshing to hear them speak openly, even if it was about something small, like that their husband snored.

Of course these women also mentioned the good things as well. But they could see both sides. And these women seemed to be returning more quickly to "regular life," much more so than the women who could only glorify their husbands.

--

This awareness helped me to "even out" my perception of things.

Walt was no saint. It seemed better to acknowledge that and face it, rather than to glorify him. Somehow, I knew that looking at the totality of my relationship with Walt was going to help me get back to "the living."

I started to spend time thinking about what I was NOT missing.

It was not an unhealthy thing for me to do.

I needed to look at "all" of Walt, and that is exactly what he would have wanted me to do.

27

HE WASN'T PERFECT

When we met, Walt was up front about himself; he told me right away that he had never felt "normal."

He had grown up in a small town and was very gifted. School was so easy for him that he often became bored and found ways to get into trouble. He was a teenager in the 50's, and they didn't have advanced classes like those that exist now.

He was most likely suffering from depression as a child, but back then, these things were not addressed.

As a teen he started drinking, as a way to "self-medicate," to cope with his turbulent mind.

Years later, he was officially diagnosed with clinical depression. He was prescribed medication, but he didn't like the way it made him feel. He refused to take any prescribed medicine; he said he would rather take the lows along with the highs, than have a flat-line personality.

I knew Walt had drinks every night after work, but it never concerned me. He never acted "drunk" or odd in any way.

He would come home from work, have a drink and say he was "taking the edge off."

I was not a drinker. With my limited experience, I believed someone only had a drinking problem if they were sloppy and falling down. Walt was always even-tempered, fully functional, and rarely missed work.

I learned that Walt had other issues; he had what was called "addictive behavior."

Addictive behavior is described as "behavior that occurs in individuals who believe they do not fit into societal norms, they act on impulses, and are driven to rebel. They continue despite negative physical and social consequences, craving relief from their mental stress."

This described him perfectly.

For Walt, in addition to his drinking, this showed up in the form of gambling, and also in excessive shopping.

The shopping was not a problem, because buying more things than we needed was not that bad – it was the gambling that was an issue.

He liked to play poker, and in my naiveté, I thought it was just like playing Black Jack in Las Vegas, just something fun to do, not an addiction.

But it was nothing like that. The sudden desire to head out to a local poker club was driven by his need to escape what was happening in his mind.

He would suddenly say he just needed to get out of the house.

This always upset me. It usually happened late at night, and once he left he was gone the entire night.

We would argue about it.

There was one time when he said he was going to go out, and I begged him not to leave. That time he didn't; he stayed home. But he was miserable.

I never asked him to stay again. I just let him go, but it always upset me.

He was driven to escape the obsessiveness in his mind.

--

There were periods of time when he would be OK.

He believed, as others with untreated depression do, that a change in circumstance would magically make his life better. I went right along believing with him.

"If only we get engaged, I'll be fine."

"Once we are married, I'll be normal."

"When we have a baby, I won't go out anymore."

None of these things were true.

This part of him was very difficult for me. It made me worry.

Sometimes I would drive to the poker club he was at and make sure his car was in the parking lot, and that he wasn't somewhere else. His car was always there, so I knew he was telling the truth. But it always hurt my feelings that he wanted to spend the entire night playing poker rather than be with me.

I did not understand that he was trying to make his life work, by balancing a high-pressure job with his addictive behavior. It really had nothing to do with me.

He didn't stop after we got engaged.

He didn't stop after we were married.

He didn't stop after I became pregnant.

He tried very hard to control his impulses after Ryan was born. But one evening when Ryan was 5 weeks old, he came in from gardening and said, "I'm going out." My heart sank. I knew he would never get over this problem.

He was gone that whole night and I never went to sleep. But I didn't follow him to the club to make sure he was there. I now had a baby to take care of and I wasn't going to go driving around with him at midnight.

Walt managed his addiction as best he could until he died, but was never successful in conquering it.

--

A few months after he died, I was thinking about how much calmer I felt without having to deal with these problems.

Then, one night, I woke up suddenly, and noticed he wasn't beside me.

I sat up, and thought, "Where is he? Is he at that stupid club?"

As I awoke fully, I realized that, no, he wasn't.

He wasn't at that club.

Because .... he was at Forest Lawn Cemetery.

I lay back down and stared at the ceiling.

I felt so guilty for having this thought.

It wasn't that I was happy that he had died.

But I would never again have to worry about where he was.

Because he would forever be at ..... Forest Lawn.

It was such a relief to be free of that worry.

--

I later found this article he had saved, titled "Depression." He knew what was wrong with him, and was forever trying to cope with it on his own.

28

A GLIMMER OF HOPE

On some level, I knew it would help me get better if I looked at all of Walt, both good and bad. But I did feel guilty doing this, because Walt never focused on my shortcomings.

Walt had loved me so completely for who I was; I had never before experienced that.

I was not too analytical for him. I was not too quiet. I was not too "anything."

To him, I was just right.

--

When we met at Rockwell during my job interview, I could tell he was funny and smart. And he seemed to be a very accepting and forgiving person.

He didn't mind that my degree was not in Engineering, but instead in Biochemistry. I recall him saying, "If you can analyze chemicals, then you'll be able to analyze data."

I left Rockwell that day feeling this huge connection to him. I did not feel attracted to him exactly, because he was so much older; that aspect just never crossed my mind. But I couldn't stop thinking about him. He seemed to know me already after just a couple hours…. how could that be?

I loved my job. We worked together everyday, and I began to know him as a person, not just as my boss. If he took a day off, the whole workday seemed different. I would miss him so much.

He was a wonderful listener and an incredibly compassionate man. He always took the side of the aggrieved or accused in any situation. He always said, "You don't know what that person has gone through in their life."

Still, I felt confused about why I felt drawn to this older man - I could not turn it off. I kept it hidden and told no one. He never approached me romantically in any way at work and was completely professional towards me.

After a few months had passed, he asked me if we could meet outside of work to discuss something. I said OK.

We went to this little place and ordered some drinks. He turned and looked directly at me, and told me that he was completely in love with me and had been for some time. He understood that it was unconventional, but our age difference didn't bother him.

He said he loved that I was deeply sensitive, and he could tell that something had hurt me long ago, something I didn't talk about. I don't know how he knew that, but it was true. My parents had been incredibly harsh with me when I was a teenager. It had made me very cautious around people.

I was drawn to his kindness and how he understood me so completely.

And Walt not only loved me, he liked me too.

We began seeing each other, but kept our relationship quiet at work.

The addictive side of his personality was apparent at times, but I was very young and didn't know about addiction and depression. So mostly I dismissed it, and learned to live with it.

Now all these years later, and after his death, I needed to acknowledge it in an effort to heal myself.

--

This addictive part of him was very difficult for me. I never knew when it would surface.

I hated it.

I could now finally admit there were some things I was not going to miss.

But the voices in my head were constantly arguing:

"Stop that! Stop thinking negative things about him. He died!"

"I know. But this is the way it was, and that part was hard."

This happened many times a day, for a long time. The negative thoughts crept in to my mind, and my kind side would want to sweep them away.

But, somewhere inside, I knew that this was the path I needed to go down to get to a better place.

Looking at all of him was helping to lead me to acceptance of his death.

I was determined not to be a lifetime member of the Grief Group; I wanted to be a part of the Living Group.

--

One day I had a sign that maybe I would be OK.

Each morning upon waking, my first thought was always, "Oh, he died."

But exactly at 4½ months, I woke up one morning and thought, "What should I make the kids for breakfast?"

Immediately after was my second thought, "Oh, he died."

"Oh, he died," had been my second thought, and not my first!

This was the smallest, teeniest, tiniest thing, and yet it was a true glimmer of hope for me.

I knew my subconscious mind was accepting my new reality, and that one day I might actually feel normal again.

This gave me hope.

29

THE PRIVATE FAN CLUB

There was something else that was helping me to adjust and get into acceptance.

--

After Walt died, there were two recurring thoughts that stood out to me:

1. No one loves me anymore.

2. No one will ever love our children the way their father had. I was now the only one.

I knew that other people in my family loved me, but it wasn't the same. No one was waiting to see me at the end of the day, to tell me they loved me and how special I was to them.

And I felt sorry for my children that they would be missing this very important gift they had lost – the precious love of their father.

--

When you have a baby with someone, the two of you instantly invent your own little Fan Club called, "Our baby is the best one that ever lived."

There are no other members of your Club, it is just the two of you.

Of course, you realize that every other couple in the world is thinking the same thing about their baby.

That's OK. You and your spouse know the truth. Your baby is the best and you can't believe you created this new little person together.

After Ryan was born, we spent our evenings making dinner and being together as a family. We marveled at our brand new son, how wonderful he was, how nice and sweet and funny he was, how beautiful his eyes were. This gushing between the two of us was an ongoing activity.

When Hannah was born, we added her to our "perfect baby" club.

When Walt would come home from work, I was usually busy with the baby, so he made it his job to immediately go help with Ryan. But he would always pass by me, give both of us a kiss, and say, "How's your daughter today, dear?"

He referred to her as "my" daughter because he knew I had wanted a girl, and it was his way of reaffirming that he had come through for me.

By Hannah's second month, the same routine continued. Walt would come home and head over to greet Ryan, but at some point he changed his question, instead saying, "How's OUR daughter today, dear?" He spent more and more time with her.

By the third month, Walt walked in the door and headed straight to wherever Hannah was and scooped her up. He would hold her in the air and smile at her and exclaim, "How is Daddy's little girl today??" She would always smile for him the most, and would wiggle with happiness.

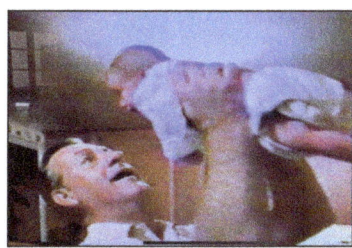

I loved watching the progression of his attachment to our little girl.

We were happy being in our little Fan Club of two, with these babies who we felt were the most perfect that were ever born.

When Walt died, I was now in our little Fan Club all by myself.

It was lonely.

There was no one else who would look at my children the same way that he and I did.

No one would hold Hannah up again and say, "How is Daddy's little girl?" No one would say, "Hi son!" to Ryan and go running after him.

My children lost half of their parental love. And I lost my counterpart.

I would now be alone in my wonderment towards them. When they reached a milestone or said something funny, if they just walked or talked or laughed…. there was no one there to glance at knowingly, smile, and think, "we have the best one."

This made me incredibly sad. It was one of the most difficult parts of losing him.

--

But, lucky for me, it turned out I had made a good decision.

My parents were now seeing my children very often and getting closer and closer to them. They understood them and adored them. My kids could do no wrong in my parents' eyes. They would tell me every funny thing they said or did. They would marvel at how special and smart they were.

At some point, it was so obvious.

My parents had joined my little Fan Club, and they looked at my kids in the same way that I did, in the same way that Walt had.

This eased some of the angst I had about my children having only one person who would love them completely.

They now had three.

Sometimes it did make me mad; it wasn't fair.

My parents had not accepted Walt as my husband, but now with him gone, they would get to watch our children grow up. And he would not.

But I learned to put those feelings aside. It wouldn't bring Walt back. I now had to do what was best for our children.

I knew Walt would be OK with any choice I made. And it was a blessing for me to no longer feel alone in my love for Ryan and Hannah. It was a gift, and helped ease my sorrow.

30

TAKING HIM WITH US

For many months, I continued with the Grief Group and began to adjust more and more to my life without Walt.

My mother was very helpful and very loving, but she was desperate to see me be "OK." She felt strongly that if I moved out of the home I shared with Walt, that I would suddenly be fine.

She started saying right away, over and over again, "You need to move out of that house!" She couldn't help herself.

But no, I couldn't. I couldn't leave yet. He was there. I would not leave him. I could feel him in every room.

When 4 or 5 months had passed, I slowly began to look through his clothes.

I started on his sock drawer. He had way too many pairs of socks. He was a bargain shopper, and if something was on sale, he bought a whole lot of whatever it was because he was "saving money." I think there were over a hundred pairs of socks in there, and yet he probably only wore the five pairs on top. I believe I kept those 5, and put the rest in a bag to donate.

That was a start.

Next, I went through his dress shirts and ties. This wasn't too hard either because he didn't like dressing up for work, it was just something he had to do. I saved a few shirts and a couple ties; I wondered if one day Ryan might wear them. I put the rest in the donation pile.

Little by little, I let his things go. He had a lot of tools. I gave those to his son-in-law.

I have no memory of what I did with his car.

--

Walt also had a lot of gardening equipment, fertilizers, and planting materials. He loved gardening. He spent every weekend out in the yard planting, pruning, and watering. It gave him great peace, and was a respite from his mind-demanding engineering job.

At first he was only growing vegetables – that's what his family had done when he was growing up. We always had corn on the cob and fresh green beans from his garden. He planted strawberries for Ryan to pick. He always took Ryan out to help him in the yard.

I asked him one day, "why don't you plant any flowers?"

"I don't know, dear, I never thought of that!" he said, and he laughed.

He knew I liked roses, so he started planting rose bushes. Sometimes he would order special seeds out of gardening catalogs that claimed they would produce blue or black colored roses. We mostly laughed at the results – they never looked the way the catalog claimed they would.

But he did grow many beautiful rose bushes. I loved them, and he took such good care of them.

--

After almost a year from his passing, I felt ready to think about moving. I had slowly given away most of his clothes and possessions.

I found a house in Long Beach located near my sister, Teresa, and only a couple miles from my parents. I knew having family close by would greatly help me, and I loved that my kids would grow up near their cousins.

When moving day came, I dug up Walt's 4 favorite rose bushes and took them with us to plant at the new house. It felt like I was bringing some of his most prized keepsakes with us, plus part of his heart; they represented what he loved to do, and what gave him joy.

We were taking him with us.

--

I planted the 4 rose bushes in our front yard where I could look at them every single day, whenever I opened my front door, and whenever I returned home.

In the time following our move, I became busy turning my new house into a home: wallpapering the kids' rooms and doing some remodeling. In a way, I felt lighter, as if I wasn't carrying as much of a burden.

I knew I had done the right thing in waiting a year though: if I had moved sooner, I don't think I would have transitioned as well to being the head of the household in this new home.

The kids were happy to be in the new neighborhood. They liked the house, and I put a swing set into our new backyard.

Ryan was now 3 ½ years old. The days of him crying when the mailman came had stopped months before. He had let go of the memory, and was a happy cheerful little boy. Hannah had only been 3 months old when her father died; now she was a content and active toddler.

I talked to them about their Daddy all the time, and showed them videos of him.

But I think, for them, Daddy became someone who just lived in the TV, someone they knew was important to Mommy, and someone who had loved them.

I knew their memories of Walt were gone. I had to accept it. I wanted them to have happy childhoods, and I could only make that happen by living in the present.

Any grieving I needed to do, I did it alone, away from them.

31

CONTINUING INTO ACCEPTANCE

On the road to acceptance, there were many times I had to forgive myself.

--

A few months after Walt died, I had picked up my video camera again. I filmed some of Hannah in her walker, but most of it was of me questioning Ryan about what he remembered about his father.

I was relentless. I put so much pressure on my son to try and remember his father, and to be a role model for his sister. Ryan tried hard to remember, but he couldn't. I would ask him questions like, "Remember when Daddy would put you in the swing?"

He didn't remember. But he tried so hard to answer the questions the way he thought I wanted him to. It's disturbing for me to watch how relentless I was, but it was a long time ago. I forgave myself.

Continuing to slowly accept his death, brought me further into living life to its fullest.

--

Some things I did were very smart.

I visited Walt's family in Spokane every year. I felt that would give our kids a sense of where he had come from, and I think it did. They remember those trips well, spending time with their paternal grandmother and their aunts.

Then, when they were 8 and 10, I took them to Kennedy Space Center in Florida to see a Space Shuttle launch. I wanted them to see what their father had worked so hard on, and it was a special memory for me because it signified how we had met working together at Rockwell.

There were times when my kids were in school when it was difficult for them not to have a father.

Ryan had a teacher in 2nd grade who asked the students to fill out this paper and answer questions about their father:

Ryan brought the completed paper home, and he had filled it in with an answer to every question. None of the answers were accurate. I asked him how he came up with these responses and he burst into tears. He didn't know how to tell the teacher that he didn't have a father to write about. I went and talked to her later, and from then on she told her students they could write about an uncle or grandfather as well.

I also learned after that, to quietly let teachers know that I was their only parent.

In general, though, my children did not like when anyone knew. People always felt bad for them and that made them uncomfortable.

Having a single mother was normal to them; they didn't feel like they were missing anything.

And, they did not miss "him", because they never really **knew** him.

They only knew "about him."

This was something I had to continually work on accepting.

--

My stepdaughters had given me this little gold heart locket when I married their father. On one side, I put a tiny picture of Walt taken on our wedding day. On the other side, I put two tiny pictures of my kids, taken around the time he died. I wanted to memorialize what they looked like at that time.

I wore that locket to every single significant event in my children's lives. I wore it to graduations. I wore it to performances. I wore it every time I needed to bring Walt with me so he could be there at this part of our children's lives.

I needed him there with me.

I would reach up and hold the locket with my right hand and close my eyes to feel his presence. I could always feel him there next to me, watching our children with pride.

--

Even years after being widowed, things would sometimes happen that would be so unexpected.

When Hannah was 14, she was in a play at school. She was so tiny in stature that she was given the role of the 7-year-old girl being raised by a single father. She needed to wear a coat for the performance; I still had one she had loved in 2nd grade, and she could still put it on – the director had cast her perfectly.

I went to see the play, and of course, I was wearing my locket.

But I was not prepared for one of the scenes.

The father in the play walks out of the room. Hannah, as the daughter, runs after the father and calls out, "Daddy, Daddy! Come back Daddy!"

I could barely breathe. I held onto the locket with both my hands.

Walt had now been gone 14 years. But I realized in that moment, that I had never before heard my little girl say those words, "Daddy! Daddy!" … because she was an infant when he died, and had not yet learned to talk.

I was surprised at my reaction. Tears poured from my eyes. I was so proud of her performance, but I was also so aware of what she had lost, even though she would never understand that.

--

Over the years, people would tell my children how sorry they were that they did not have a father.

One time, when my son was a grown man, I heard him answer someone in this way:

"Thank you, but that was my Mom's tragedy, not ours, because we don't remember."

It was his way of answering the person honestly, always believing that he had not suffered, and yet not diminishing what he knew I had gone through.

--

My son would say that he had never lost anything because he did not remember.

But I remembered.

He had only been 2½, but his father spent hours with him every evening, and all day on weekends. They went on walks together, worked in the garden together, took out the trashcans together, and went to the store together.

I remembered the days and weeks when the mailman would come. Our son cried every time. He didn't understand where Daddy was, and why he couldn't come home anymore. He had missed him so much.

It was definitely a loss for him.

--

At the time I wrote this memoir, Ryan was 33 years old, the exact age I was when his father died. He did not know many parts of the story, because I had stopped talking about it years ago.

I think he finally realized that he actually had lost something, someone, even though he didn't remember.

My son's kindness and admiration for me, and what I went through, was just an incredible gift.

Hannah was equally grateful and kind as she read these stories.

32

THE OPPORTUNITY

For a few years I was at peace being a full-time mother. I was happy that I did not have to return to work after losing Walt. He had a pension and I received social security benefits.

But I hadn't really noticed that there were parts of me that I had filed away and silently put on hold. I pushed them way down where they would not be seen or dealt with.

Some of them:

- Being a woman

- Using creativity

- Exerting intelligence

- Learning new things

These were all quietly filed away and waiting for my attention.

After a couple years at the new house, an interesting opportunity presented itself.

Initially it seemed like nothing, but then turned into absolutely everything.

--

One evening my father called. He had made a bad business decision, trusted the wrong person, and invested in something he knew nothing about. He wanted me to help him.

Having no experience in this type of situation, I honestly didn't see how I could help.

He said that didn't matter to him, he really needed me there the next day.

OK.

The next afternoon I put on a dress. I realized I hadn't worn a dress in a couple years. Hmmmmm.

I showed up at my father's new business venture, a restaurant, named Caffe La Strada.

Everything there was busy and buzzing, people moved here and there.

My father's evil business partner was glaring at me. The two of them were not getting along, and he was not happy I was there observing.

I didn't know what I was doing at first, but I understood that I was a mental reinforcement there for my father. He needed me.

--

Something happened within me on that night.

I started to feel alive.

I started to feel challenged.

Parts of me were waking up; it was like they were all screaming at me: Let us out!

That night helped me to begin reclaiming all of those buried parts of myself. I hadn't even realized they were missing, until they all came flooding back.

In the weeks and months that followed, I worked in the evenings at my father's restaurant. I hadn't planned on going back to work for a while: this was an unexpected opportunity. I did not know where it would lead, but it felt good to be working in some way again.

I still felt like a full-time Mom because it was not a daylong job of many hours away from my kids. We spent every day together: I dropped them off and picked them up from school, they spent the afternoons on their homework and art projects, and we continued fixing up our new home.

In the evenings I would drop the kids at my parents' house, and they were so excited to go there every night.

This was how they developed such a strong bond with their grandparents.

It was a true blessing, and a scenario that I never could have predicted.

--

In those couple years of working at the restaurant, there were court cases filed on both sides between my father and his partner. My father regretted that he had opened a business with such an unscrupulous person. He often said, "This was the worst business decision I have ever made."

He had a difficult time accepting his mistake.

In the end, my father was awarded ownership of the restaurant by the court.

My father asked me if I still wanted to keep running it, otherwise he was going to close it. I thought about it.

I was now fairly used to this routine of working in the evenings, and being home in the daytime hours. If I returned to an engineering job, I would have to find childcare for my kids every single day.

I told my father, yes, I would try running it for a while, and would see what would come of it.

I only had this very limited restaurant experience during the partnership dispute. I knew if I wanted it to be successful, I would have to learn a lot more about business.

I visited other restaurant owners and asked their advice. I hired a restaurant consultant and asked for suggestions. I went to the bookstore and bought books on marketing and managing a business. I took seminars to learn all I could.

Within a few years, I changed the name to simply "La Strada," and I had turned it into a healthy thriving business. Along the way, I paid my father back his original investment.

La Strada was mine.

My father continued to say that going into business with that partner was "the worst business decision he had ever made."

One day I looked at him and said, "Your worst decision, was the best thing that ever happened to me." He nearly cried.

It had helped bring me back to life.

33

REAL ACCEPTANCE

Eventually, my life evened out and things got better. I could finally wake up each day with gratitude and some sense of peace.

I balanced work and being a single Mom. I volunteered many hours at my kids' school.

We stayed in that home in Long Beach for 14 years.

When the kids were teenagers, we moved to another area in the city that was closer to my business and to my parents, who were now older and needing some assistance.

I again brought Walt's 4 rose bushes with me to the next house, and they have been planted by my front door for 15 years now.

I owned and operated my restaurant for 27 years. I loved it, but I closed it in 2020, it was time for a change.

--

I dated and had significant relationships over the years, but I never remarried. I think I would have liked to, but somehow I could never make that part of my life work out.

Those first few years I was working through my grief and acceptance.

And when my kids were young, it wasn't easy to fit in time for dating, or to find someone who was OK dating a single mother with 2 kids.

Owning a restaurant was a drawback as well to meeting someone. I had what I called a "flip-flop schedule:" I was home during the day, and I worked every night.

I still hope to find a Mr. Right. He will never be Walt, and that is OK with me. Above all I want to find someone who gave me the two things that Walt did: he understood me, and loved me for who I was.

--

Our son, Ryan, graduated from UC Berkeley with a degree in Economics. He worked for a commercial real estate firm for 9 years, and is now an entrepreneur creating custom hats in New York City, where he has lived for the last 10 years. He has the same fearless personality as his father.

Our daughter, Hannah, graduated from UC Berkeley also, recently earned her law degree, and is a practicing attorney in Santa Monica. She loves grocery stores, the same way her father did, and can spend hours there shopping.

They both still have their huge blue eyes, and so many other characteristics of their father's. They are both incredibly bright, and very compassionate.

They know and understand who he was. They are incredibly grateful to me for being their mother, and I treasure that they show me this kindness.

I fervently believe the greatest gift we can give to our departed loved ones is a life fully lived. I strived for that every day, and I continue to do so.

--

I think I honored the promise I made to Walt that day in the emergency room, when I looked at his blue eyes for the last time, and told him I would take care of our children.

I think he would be so proud of me.

I love you honey. Love, Lisa

34

THOUGHTS ON GRIEVING

I can't pinpoint just one thing that got me back to the Land of the Living, but here are some things that worked for me:

#1 Take Your Time

Don't let anyone rush you. Only give away your loved one's things when you are ready.

Let people know that it is important for you to talk about your loved one. They will change the subject to "get your mind off it." They don't understand that that is all you are thinking about. Just say gently, "do you mind if I just talk about him/her a little longer?" They will be happy to listen. They just don't know.

#2 The Nights will Get Better

It will take awhile for the dreaded 3AM routine to go away, when you wake up and relive your tragedy. The wondering of what you could have done differently, or why this was the fate that was handed to you, is just tortuous. But it will lessen, I promise.

Look for signs that you might one day be OK. There will come a day, when a "new thought" will be your first thought upon awakening.

Then, your second thought will be, "Oh, he died."

But this tiny little thing will mean that your subconscious is starting to accept what happened.

#3 Be Determined

I was determined to get better. For myself and for my kids, I needed to return to the life of the living, to be a person who lived life to the fullest. Being a mother was a big part of this determination: it motivated me to create the best life I could for my children.

#4 Be Willing

Try anything to get past that hopeless feeling that everything is a lost cause. I wanted to wake up and greet each day with enthusiasm and gratitude instead of sadness and despair. I believe my desperation greatly assisted me in being willing to try so many things: the Grief Group, exercise, therapy, reading, volunteering, etc. I did it all.

#5 Accept Help

Accept help when offered. Your loved one is sending you these helpers.

I know how difficult this can be to do. I'm very independent, and I wanted to prove that I could do it all on my own. But that doesn't lead to any type of sanity or solace.

#6 Join a Grief Group

Find a support group. Look around at those attending. Notice the people that seem to be finding their way back to life, and do what they do. Be determined not to be a lifelong member of the group - your loved one would not want that for you.

#7 Do Things you were Going to do Together

Go do those things that you know your loved one would want you to do. Go on that trip you planned to take together. There will be times when you suddenly feel their presence - they will be smiling down upon you with so much pride that you carried on, even without them.

This is what they want. You will feel such emotion in these moments - both joy, and deep sorrow. But you will also feel so alive, and so very grateful.

Your loved one is telling you they are OK. Try to believe it.

#8 Look at the Whole Picture

This can feel disloyal at first, but for me, it helped. The people in the Grief Group the longest were the ones who could only idolize their spouses. Those who spoke freely about all aspects of their departed spouse, seemed to be moving into acceptance more quickly. Somehow, for me, acknowledging that he was a human being with both wonderful qualities, and character flaws, helped me to accept that death was part of being human.

#9 Try to Accept it

I had asked many times, "Why did he have to die?" But I knew why. I had known deep down inside, but couldn't face it for a long time. I felt protective of him and did not want to have negative thoughts about him.

But once I started accepting the truth, I started to feel like my old self was returning.

#10 Notice the Kindnesses

Take note of even the smallest kindnesses along the way, from people trying to help or assist you. These are things you will never forget because, no matter how small or insignificant they may seem, they are a continuing reminder of the beauty of humanity.

I never ever forgot these acts of kindness; they lifted me up, over and over again.

#11 Celebrate the Joy

Try to focus on the joy your loved one brought to the world. Read the cards and letters and messages from people who wrote to let you know what a difference your loved one made in their life. Read them again.

Look for the little signs of improvement that show you are getting there, like waking up without having a bad dream, or going to the store without crying.

One day, all you will see when you wake up everyday, is the joy your loved one gave to you and to the world.

--

The best ending is to find peace.

I found it.

I loved Walt, I always will. He gave me the beautiful gifts of Ryan and Hannah, and of unconditional love.

I'm not mad at how he chose to live his life. He did his best and was true to himself.

Be true to yourself.

I promise you, you will be better one day.

LOVE FROM RYAN

A Tribute from Ryan, written when I closed my restaurant, La Strada, in 2020:

27 years ago my mother helped my grandfather open an Italian restaurant, and after 27 epic years, this past weekend was the final one for La Strada.

My mother had previously been a rocket scientist and worked on the space shuttle programs where she met my father. My father passed suddenly from a heart attack when I was 2, and my sister was 3 months old. She decided to help my grandfather with the restaurant so she could have a more flexible schedule to raise my sister and me as a young single mother.

La Strada was our second home, a place where countless young adults called Lisa their other mom. It wasn't just a restaurant; it was an icon that touched so many lives in our community over nearly three decades. My mom has sacrificed so much to make La Strada a special place, and a safe place to influence and improve the lives of others. I have tried to emulate this same experience with my hat shop in NYC.

My Mom made this very difficult and emotional decision, because she's a badass and has other things she wants to accomplish in the next chapter of her life.

My mom is a rock star, my hero, and the strongest person I know. She is the OG vibe shepherd, and everything I've been able to do in my life is because of her love, support and guidance.

I love you mama.

LOVE FROM HANNAH

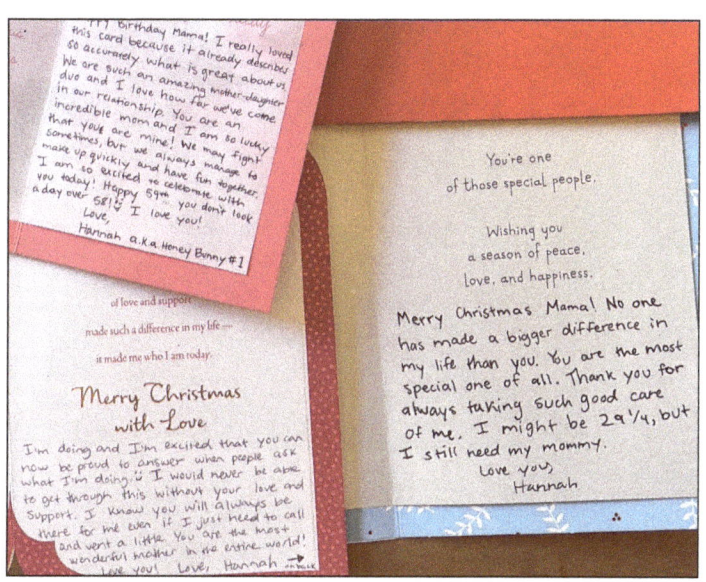

ABOUT THE AUTHOR

Lisa Ramelow recently finished a successful 27-year run in the restaurant business. She served up Italian food, and always joked that she was "cheating" because she is not Italian and she cannot cook.

She never thought of her job as serving food; instead she considered it to be "mentoring young people" (her beloved employees).

For 10 years she has also been writing real-life stories about everything from her business, to community activism, to stories about her beautiful shoe collection. Her stories are well followed, and are mostly told with love, self-deprecation, and humor.

Now that she has finished her restaurant career, she is busy putting her unique stories into book form. She resides in sunny southern California, and is always looking for joy and unique experiences to write about.

Keep in touch with Lisa via the web:

Website: https://www.akindnessiwillneverforget.com

https:/www.LisaRamelow.com

Facebook: https://www.facebook.com/LisaLaStrada

Instagram: https://www.instagram.com/lisaramelow/

www.ingramcontent.com/pod-product-compliance
Lightning Source LLC
Chambersburg PA
CBHW042011060526
44119CB00112B/206